PENGUIN ARCHIVE

To Read and Dream

Christina Rossetti

1830–1894

A PENGUIN SINCE 2001

Christina Rossetti
To Read and Dream

PENGUIN ARCHIVE

PENGUIN BOOKS

UK | USA | Canada | Ireland | Australia
India | New Zealand | South Africa

Penguin Books is part of the Penguin Random House group of companies whose addresses can be found at global.penguinrandomhouse.com

Penguin Random House UK,
One Embassy Gardens, 8 Viaduct Gardens, London SW11 7BW

penguin.co.uk

Complete Poems published in Penguin Classics 2001; *Selected Poems* published 2008
This selection published in Penguin Classics 2025

003

Text copyright © Louisiana State University Press, 1979, 1986, 1990

No part of this book may be used or reproduced in any manner for the purpose of training artificial intelligence technologies or systems. In accordance with Article 4(3) of the DSM Directive 2019/790, Penguin Random House expressly reserves this work from the text and data mining exception.

Set in 10.8/13.75pt Dante MT Std
Typeset by Jouve (UK), Milton Keynes
Printed and bound in Great Britain by Clays Ltd, Elcograf S.p.A.

The authorized representative in the EEA is Penguin Random House Ireland, Morrison Chambers, 32 Nassau Street, Dublin D02 YH68

A CIP catalogue record for this book is available from the British Library

ISBN: 978–0–241–74723–0

Penguin Random House is committed to a sustainable future for our business, our readers and our planet. This book is made from Forest Stewardship Council® certified paper.

Contents

'When I am dead, my dearest'	1
Remember	2
On the Death of a Cat	3
Sappho	5
Have you forgotten?	6
Heart's Chill Between	7
Death's Chill Between	9
A Pause of Thought	11
On Keats	12
Dream-Land	13
The World	15
From the Antique	16
Three Stages	17
Echo	21
Shut Out	22
In an Artist's Studio	24
Winter: My Secret	25
At Home	27
L.E.L.	29

Goblin Market	31
The Queen of Hearts	51
Beauty Is Vain	53
A Birthday	54
Memory	55
A Smile and a Sigh	57
Autumn Violets	58
'They Desire a Better Country'	59
Confluents	61
'Hollow-sounding and Mysterious'	63
At Last	65
The Thread of Life	66
Touching 'Never'	68
An Old-World Thicket	69
Another Spring	77
'Redeeming the Time'	78
A Castle-Builder's World	79
Three Seasons	82
One Day	83
An Apple Gathering	84
Grown and Flown	86
A Farm Walk	87
Somewhere or Other	90

'The Iniquity of the Fathers upon the Children'	91
Love Lies Bleeding	110
A Bird's Song	111
Bird Raptures	112
The Key-Note	113
Winter Rain	114
The Lowest Room	116
My Dream	128
Gone for Ever	131
An End	132

'When I am dead, my dearest'

When I am dead, my dearest,
   Sing no sad songs for me;
Plant thou no roses at my head,
   Nor shady cypress tree:
Be the green grass above me
   With showers and dewdrops wet;
And if thou wilt, remember,
   And if thou wilt, forget.

I shall not see the shadows,
   I shall not feel the rain;
I shall not hear the nightingale
   Sing on, as if in pain:
And dreaming through the twilight
   That doth not rise nor set,
Haply I may remember,
   And haply may forget.

Remember

Remember me when I am gone away,
    Gone far away into the silent land;
    When you can no more hold me by the hand,
Nor I half turn to go yet turning stay.
Remember me when no more day by day
    You tell me of our future that you planned:
    Only remember me; you understand
It will be late to counsel then or pray.
Yet if you should forget me for a while
    And afterwards remember, do not grieve:
    For if the darkness and corruption leave
    A vestige of the thoughts that once I had,
Better by far you should forget and smile
    Than that you should remember and be sad.

On the Death of a Cat

A Friend of Mine, Aged Ten Years and a Half.

Who shall tell the lady's grief
When her Cat was past relief?
Who shall number the hot tears
Shed o'er her, beloved for years?
Who shall say the dark dismay
Which her dying caused that day?

Come, ye Muses, one and all,
Come obedient to my call.
Come and mourn, with tuneful breath,
Each one for a separate death
And while you in numbers sigh,
I will sing her elegy.

Of a noble race she came,
And Grimalkin was her name.
Young and old full many a mouse
Felt the prowess of her house:
Weak and strong full many a rat
Cowered beneath her crushing pat:
And the birds around the place
Shrank from her too close embrace.
But one night, reft of her strength,
She laid down and died at length:
Lay a kitten by her side,

In whose life the mother died.
Spare her line and lineage,
Guard her kitten's tender age,
And that kitten's name as wide
Shall be known as her's that died.

Sappho

I sigh at day-dawn, and I sigh
When the dull day is passing by.
I sigh at evening, and again
I sigh when night brings sleep to men.
Oh! it were better far to die
Than thus for ever mourn and sigh,
And in death's dreamless sleep to be
Unconscious that none weep for me;
Eased from my weight of heaviness,
Forgetful of forgetfulness,
Resting from pain and care and sorrow
Thro' the long night that knows no morrow;
Living unloved, to die unknown,
Unwept, untended and alone.

Have you forgotten?

Have you forgotten how one Summer night
    We wandered forth together with the moon,
    While warm winds hummed to us a sleepy tune?
Have you forgotten how you praised both light
And darkness; not embarrassed yet not quite
    At ease? and how you said the glare of noon
    Less pleased you than the stars? but very soon
You blushed, and seemed to doubt if you were right.
We wandered far and took no note of time;
    Till on the air there came the distant call
Of church bells: we turned hastily, and yet
Ere we reached home sounded a second chime.
    But what; have you indeed forgotten all?
Ah how then is it I cannot forget?

Heart's Chill Between

I did not chide him, tho' I knew
    That he was false to me:
Chide the exhaling of the dew,
    The ebbing of the sea,
The fading of a rosy hue,
    But not inconstancy.

Why strive for love when love is o'er?
    Why bind a restive heart?
He never knew the pain I bore
    In saying: 'We must part;
Let us be friends, and nothing more':—
    Oh woman's shallow art!

But it is over, it is done;
    I hardly heed it now;
So many weary years have run
    Since then, I think not how
Things might have been; but greet each one
    With an unruffled brow.

What time I am where others be
    My heart seems very calm,
Stone calm; but if all go from me
    There comes a vague alarm,
A shrinking in the memory
    From some forgotten harm.

And often thro' the long long night
    Waking when none are near,
I feel my heart beat fast with fright,
    Yet know not what I fear.
Oh how I long to see the light
    And the sweet birds to hear!

To have the sun upon my face,
    To look up through the trees,
To walk forth in the open space,
    And listen to the breeze,
And not to dream the burial place
    Is clogging my weak knees.

Sometimes I can nor weep nor pray,
    But am half stupified;
And then all those who see me say
    Mine eyes are opened wide,
And that my wits seem gone away:—
    Ah would that I had died!

Would I could die and be at peace,
    Or living could forget;
My grief nor grows nor doth decrease,
    But ever is:—and yet
Methinks now that all this shall cease
    Before the sun shall set.

Death's Chill Between

Chide not; let me breathe a little,
   For I shall not mourn him long.
Tho' the life-cord was so brittle
   The love-cord was very strong.
I would wake a little space
Till I find a sleeping-place.

You can go, I shall not weep;
   You can go unto your rest;
My heart-ache is all too deep,
   And too sore my throbbing breast.
Can sobs be, or angry tears,
Where are neither hopes nor fears?

Tho' with you I am alone,
   And must be so everywhere,
I will make no useless moan;
   None shall say: 'She could not bear;'
While life lasts I will be strong,
But I shall not struggle long.

Listen, listen! everywhere
   A low voice is calling me,
And a step is on the stair,
   And one comes ye do not see.
Listen, listen! evermore
A dim hand knocks at the door.

Hear me: he is come again;
    My own dearest is come back.
Bring him in from the cold rain;
    Bring wine, and let nothing lack.
Thou and I will rest together,
Love, until the sunny weather.

I will shelter thee from harm,
    Hide thee from all heaviness;
Come to me, and keep thee warm
    By my side in quietness.
I will lull thee to thy sleep
With sweet songs; we will not weep.

Who hath talked of weeping? yet
    There is something at my heart
Gnawing, I would fain forget,
    And an aching and a smart—
Ah my Mother, 'tis in vain,
For he is not come again.

A Pause of Thought

I looked for that which is not, nor can be,
    And hope deferred made my heart sick in truth:
    But years must pass before a hope of youth
        Is resigned utterly.

I watched and waited with a steadfast will:
    And though the object seemed to flee away
    That I so longed for, ever day by day
        I watched and waited still.

Sometimes I said: This thing shall be no more;
    My expectation wearies and shall cease;
    I will resign it now and be at peace:
        Yet never gave it o'er.

Sometimes I said: It is an empty name
    I long for; to a name why should I give
    The peace of all the days I have to live?—
        Yet gave it all the same.

Alas, thou foolish one! alike unfit
    For healthy joy and salutary pain:
    Thou knowest the chase useless, and again
        Turnest to follow it.

On Keats

A garden in a garden: a green spot
    Where all is green: most fitting slumber-place
   For the strong man grown weary of a race
Soon over. Unto him a goodly lot
Hath fallen in fertile ground; there thorns are not,
    But his own daisies: silence, full of grace,
    Surely hath shed a quiet on his face:
His earth is but sweet leaves that fall and rot.
What was his record of himself, ere he
    Went from us? *Here lies one whose name was writ
    In water:* while the chilly shadows flit
       Of sweet Saint Agnes' Eve; while basil springs,
       His name, in every humble heart that sings,
Shall be a fountain of love, verily.

Dream-Land

Where sunless rivers weep
Their waves into the deep,
She sleeps a charmèd sleep:
    Awake her not.
Led by a single star,
She came from very far
To seek where shadows are
    Her pleasant lot.

She left the rosy morn,
She left the fields of corn,
For twilight cold and lorn
    And water springs.
Thro' sleep, as thro' a veil,
She sees the sky look pale,
And hears the nightingale
    That sadly sings.

Rest, rest, a perfect rest
Shed over brow and breast;
Her face is toward the west,
    The purple land.
She cannot see the grain
Ripening on hill and plain;
She cannot feel the rain
    Upon her hand.

Rest, rest, for evermore
Upon a mossy shore;
Rest, rest at the heart's core
   Till time shall cease:
Sleep that no pain shall wake;
Night that no morn shall break,
Till joy shall overtake
   Her perfect peace.

The World

By day she woos me, soft, exceeding fair:
    But all night as the moon so changeth she;
    Loathsome and foul with hideous leprosy
And subtle serpents gliding in her hair.
By day she wooes me to the outer air,
    Ripe fruits, sweet flowers, and full satiety:
    But thro' the night, a beast she grins at me,
A very monster void of love and prayer.
By day she stands a lie: by night she stands
    In all the naked horror of the truth
With pushing horns and clawed and clutching hands.
Is this a friend indeed; that I should sell
    My soul to her, give her my life and youth,
Till my feet, cloven too, take hold on hell?

From the Antique

It's a weary life, it is; she said:—
    Doubly blank in a woman's lot:
I wish and I wish I were a man;
    Or, better than any being, were not:

Were nothing at all in all the world,
    Not a body and not a soul;
Not so much as a grain of dust
    Or drop of water from pole to pole.

Still the world would wag on the same,
    Still the seasons go and come;
Blossoms bloom as in days of old,
    Cherries ripen and wild bees hum.

None would miss me in all the world,
    How much less would care or weep:
I should be nothing; while all the rest
    Would wake and weary and fall asleep.

Three Stages

1.

I looked for that which is not, nor can be,
    And hope deferred made my heart sick in truth;
    But years must pass before a hope of youth
        Is resigned utterly.

I watched and waited with a steadfast will:
    And though the object seemed to flee away
    That I so longed for; ever, day by day,
        I watched and waited still.

Sometimes I said: This thing shall be no more:
    My expectation wearies and shall cease;
    I will resign it now and be at peace:—
        Yet never gave it o'er.

Sometimes I said: It is an empty name
    I long for; to a name why should I give
    The peace of all the days I have to live?—
        Yet gave it all the same.

Alas, thou foolish one! alike unfit
    For healthy joy and salutary pain;
    Thou knowest the chase useless, and again
        Turnest to follow it.

2.

My happy dream is finished with,
    My dream in which alone I lived so long.
My heart slept—woe is me, it wakeneth;
        Was weak—I thought it strong.

Oh weary wakening from a life-true dream:
    Oh pleasant dream from which I wake in pain:
I rested all my trust on things that seem,
        And all my trust is vain.

I must pull down my palace that I built,
    Dig up the pleasure-gardens of my soul;
Must change my laughter to sad tears for guilt,
        My freedom to control.

Now all the cherished secrets of my heart,
    Now all my hidden hopes are turned to sin:
Part of my life is dead, part sick, and part
        Is all on fire within.

The fruitless thought of what I might have been
    Haunting me ever will not let me rest:
A cold north wind has withered all my green,
        My sun is in the west.

But where my palace stood, with the same stone,
    I will uprear a shady hermitage;
And there my spirit shall keep house alone,
        Accomplishing its age:

There other garden beds shall lie around
    Full of sweet-briar and incense-bearing thyme;
There I will sit, and listen for the sound
    Of the last lingering chime.

3.

I thought to deal the death-stroke at a blow,
    To give all, once for all, but nevermore;—
    Then sit to hear the low waves fret the shore,
        Or watch the silent snow.

'Oh rest,' I thought, 'in silence and the dark;
    Oh rest, if nothing else, from head to feet:
    Though I may see no more the poppied wheat,
        Or sunny soaring lark.

'These chimes are slow, but surely strike at last;
    This sand is slow, but surely droppeth thro';
    And much there is to suffer, much to do,
        Before the time be past.

'So will I labour, but will not rejoice:
    Will do and bear, but will not hope again;
    Gone dead alike to pulses of quick pain,
        And pleasure's counterpoise:'

I said so in my heart, and so I thought
    My life would lapse, a tedious monotone:
    I thought to shut myself, and dwell alone
        Unseeking and unsought.

But first I tired, and then my care grew slack;
   Till my heart slumbered, maybe wandered too:—
   I felt the sunshine glow again, and knew
     The swallow on its track;

All birds awoke to building in the leaves,
   All buds awoke to fulness and sweet scent,
   Ah, too, my heart woke unawares, intent
     Oh fruitful harvest sheaves.

Full pulse of life, that I had deemed was dead,
   Full throb of youth, that I had deemed at rest,—
   Alas, I cannot build myself a nest,
     I cannot crown my head

With royal purple blossoms for the feast,
   Nor flush with laughter, nor exult in song;—
   These joys may drift, as time now drifts along;
     And cease, as once they ceased.

I may pursue, and yet may not attain,
   Athirst and panting all the days I live:
   Or seem to hold, yet nerve myself to give
     What once I gave, again.

Echo

Come to me in the silence of the night;
   Come in the speaking silence of a dream;
Come with soft rounded cheeks and eyes as bright
   As sunlight on a stream;
     Come back in tears,
O memory, hope, love of finished years.

Oh dream how sweet, too sweet, too bitter sweet,
   Whose wakening should have been in Paradise,
Where souls brimfull of love abide and meet;
   Where thirsting longing eyes
     Watch the slow door
That opening, letting in, lets out no more.

Yet come to me in dreams, that I may live
   My very life again tho' cold in death:
Come back to me in dreams, that I may give
   Pulse for pulse, breath for breath:
     Speak low, lean low,
As long ago, my love, how long ago.

Shut Out

The door was shut. I looked between
   Its iron bars; and saw it lie,
   My garden, mine, beneath the sky,
Pied with all flowers bedewed and green:

From bough to bough the song-birds crossed,
   From flower to flower the moths and bees;
   With all its nests and stately trees
It had been mine, and it was lost.

A shadowless spirit kept the gate,
   Blank and unchanging like the grave.
   I peering thro' said: 'Let me have
Some buds to cheer my outcast state.'

He answered not. 'Or give me, then,
   But one small twig from shrub or tree;
   And bid my home remember me
Until I come to it again.'

The spirit was silent; but he took
   Mortar and stone to build a wall;
   He left no loophole great or small
Thro' which my straining eyes might look:

So now I sit here quite alone
    Blinded with tears; nor grieve for that,
    For nought is left worth looking at
Since my delightful land is gone.

A violet bed is budding near,
    Wherein a lark has made her nest:
    And good they are, but not the best;
And dear they are, but not so dear.

In an Artist's Studio

One face looks out from all his canvasses,
    One selfsame figure sits or walks or leans;
    We found her hidden just behind those screens,
That mirror gave back all her loveliness.
A queen in opal or in ruby dress,
    A nameless girl in freshest summer greens,
    A saint, an angel;—every canvass means
The same one meaning, neither more nor less.
He feeds upon her face by day and night,
    And she with true kind eyes looks back on him
Fair as the moon and joyful as the light:
    Not wan with waiting, not with sorrow dim;
Not as she is, but was when hope shone bright;
    Not as she is, but as she fills his dream.

Winter: My Secret

I tell my secret? No indeed, not I:
Perhaps some day, who knows?
But not today; it froze, and blows, and snows,
And you're too curious: fie!
You want to hear it? well:
Only, my secret's mine, and I won't tell.

Or, after all, perhaps there's none:
Suppose there is no secret after all,
But only just my fun.
Today's a nipping day, a biting day;
In which one wants a shawl,
A veil, a cloak, and other wraps:
I cannot ope to every one who taps,
And let the draughts come whistling thro' my hall;
Come bounding and surrounding me,
Come buffeting, astounding me,
Nipping and clipping thro' my wraps and all.
I wear my mask for warmth: who ever shows
His nose to Russian snows
To be pecked at by every wind that blows?
You would not peck? I thank you for good will,
Believe, but leave that truth untested still.
Spring's an expansive time: yet I don't trust
March with its peck of dust,
Nor April with its rainbow-crowned brief showers,

Nor even May, whose flowers
One frost may wither thro' the sunless hours.

Perhaps some languid summer day,
When drowsy birds sing less and less,
And golden fruit is ripening to excess,
If there's not too much sun nor too much cloud,
And the warm wind is neither still nor loud,
Perhaps my secret I may say,
Or you may guess.

At Home

When I was dead, my spirit turned
    To seek the much frequented house:
I passed the door, and saw my friends
    Feasting beneath green orange boughs;
From hand to hand they pushed the wine,
    They sucked the pulp of plum and peach;
They sang, they jested, and they laughed,
        For each was loved of each.

I listened to their honest chat:
    Said one: 'Tomorrow we shall be
Plod plod along the featureless sands
    And coasting miles and miles of sea.'
Said one: 'Before the turn of tide
    We will achieve the eyrie-seat.'
Said one: 'Tomorrow shall be like
        Today, but much more sweet.'

'Tomorrow,' said they, strong with hope,
    And dwelt upon the pleasant way:
'Tomorrow,' cried they one and all,
    While no one spoke of yesterday.
Their life stood full at blessed noon;
    I, only I, had passed away:
'Tomorrow and today,' they cried;
        I was of yesterday.

I shivered comfortless, but cast
    No chill across the tablecloth;
I all-forgotten shivered, sad
    To stay and yet to part how loth:
I passed from the familiar room,
    I who from love had passed away,
Like the remembrance of a guest
    That tarrieth but a day.

L.E.L.

'Whose heart was breaking for a little love.'

Downstairs I laugh, I sport and jest with all:
    But in my solitary room above
I turn my face in silence to the wall;
    My heart is breaking for a little love.
        Tho' winter frosts are done,
        And birds pair every one,
And leaves peep out, for springtide is begun.

I feel no spring, while spring is wellnigh blown,
    I find no nest, while nests are in the grove:
Woe's me for mine own heart that dwells alone,
    My heart that breaketh for a little love.
        While golden in the sun
        Rivulets rise and run,
While lilies bud, for springtide is begun.

All love, are loved, save only I; their hearts
    Beat warm with love and joy, beat full thereof:
They cannot guess, who play the pleasant parts,
    My heart is breaking for a little love.
        While beehives wake and whirr,
        And rabbit thins his fur,
In living spring that sets the world astir.

I deck myself with silks and jewelry,
   I plume myself like any mated dove:
They praise my rustling show, and never see
   My heart is breaking for a little love.
      While sprouts green lavender
      With rosemary and myrrh,
For in quick spring the sap is all astir.

Perhaps some saints in glory guess the truth,
   Perhaps some angels read it as they move,
And cry one to another full of ruth,
   'Her heart is breaking for a little love.'
      Tho' other things have birth,
      And leap and sing for mirth,
When springtime wakes and clothes and feeds the earth.

Yet saith a saint: 'Take patience for thy scathe;'
   Yet saith an angel: 'Wait, for thou shalt prove
True best is last, true life is born of death,
   O thou, heart-broken for a little love.
Then love shall fill thy girth,
      And love make fat thy dearth,
      When new spring builds new heaven and clean new earth.'

Goblin Market

Morning and evening
Maids heard the goblins cry:
'Come buy our orchard fruits,
Come buy, come buy:
Apples and quinces,
Lemons and oranges,
Plump unpecked cherries,
Melons and raspberries,
Bloom-down-cheeked peaches,
Swart-headed mulberries,
Wild free-born cranberries,
Crab-apples, dewberries,
Pine-apples, blackberries,
Apricots, strawberries;—
All ripe together
In summer weather,—
Morns that pass by,
Fair eves that fly;
Come buy, come buy:
Our grapes fresh from the vine,
Pomegranates full and fine,
Dates and sharp bullaces,
Rare pears and greengages,
Damsons and bilberries,
Taste them and try:
Currants and gooseberries,
Bright-fire-like barberries,

Figs to fill your mouth,
Citrons from the South,
Sweet to tongue and sound to eye;
Come buy, come buy.'

Evening by evening
Among the brookside rushes,
Laura bowed her head to hear,
Lizzie veiled her blushes:
Crouching close together
In the cooling weather,
With clasping arms and cautioning lips,
With tingling cheeks and finger tips.
'Lie close,' Laura said,
Pricking up her golden head:
'We must not look at goblin men,
We must not buy their fruits:
Who knows upon what soil they fed
Their hungry thirsty roots?'
'Come buy,' call the goblins
Hobbling down the glen.
'Oh,' cried Lizzie, 'Laura, Laura,
You should not peep at goblin men.'
Lizzie covered up her eyes,
Covered close lest they should look;
Laura reared her glossy head,
And whispered like the restless brook:
'Look, Lizzie, look, Lizzie,
Down the glen tramp little men.
One hauls a basket,
One bears a plate,

One lugs a golden dish
Of many pounds weight.
How fair the vine must grow
Whose grapes are so luscious;
How warm the wind must blow
Thro' those fruit bushes.'
'No,' said Lizzie: 'No, no, no;
Their offers should not charm us,
Their evil gifts would harm us.'

She thrust a dimpled finger
In each ear, shut eyes and ran:
Curious Laura chose to linger
Wondering at each merchant man.
One had a cat's face,
One whisked a tail,
One tramped at a rat's pace,
One crawled like a snail,
One like a wombat prowled obtuse and furry,
One like a ratel tumbled hurry skurry.
She heard a voice like voice of doves
Cooing all together:
They sounded kind and full of loves
In the pleasant weather.

Laura stretched her gleaming neck
Like a rush-imbedded swan,
Like a lily from the beck,
Like a moonlit poplar branch,
Like a vessel at the launch
When its last restraint is gone.

Backwards up the mossy glen
Turned and trooped the goblin men,
With their shrill repeated cry,
'Come buy, come buy.'
When they reached where Laura was
They stood stock still upon the moss,
Leering at each other,
Brother with queer brother;
Signalling each other,
Brother with sly brother.
One set his basket down,
One reared his plate;
One began to weave a crown

Of tendrils, leaves and rough nuts brown
(Men sell not such in any town);
One heaved the golden weight
Of dish and fruit to offer her:
'Come buy, come buy,' was still their cry.
Laura stared but did not stir,
Longed but had no money:
The whisk-tailed merchant bade her taste
In tones as smooth as honey,
The cat-faced purr'd,
The rat-paced spoke a word
Of welcome, and the snail-paced even was heard;
One parrot-voiced and jolly
Cried 'Pretty Goblin' still for 'Pretty Polly;'—
One whistled like a bird.

But sweet-tooth Laura spoke in haste.
'Good folk, I have no coin;
To take were to purloin:
I have no copper in my purse,
I have no silver either,
And all my gold is on the furze
That shakes in windy weather
Above the rusty heather.'
'You have much gold upon your head,'
They answered all together:
'Buy from us with a golden curl.'
She clipped a precious golden lock,
She dropped a tear more rare than pearl,
Then sucked their fruit globes fair or red:
Sweeter than honey from the rock,
Stronger than man-rejoicing wine,
Clearer than water flowed that juice;
She never tasted such before,
How should it cloy with length of use?
She sucked and sucked and sucked the more
Fruits which that unknown orchard bore;
She sucked until her lips were sore;

Then flung the emptied rinds away
But gathered up one kernel-stone,
And knew not was it night or day
As she turned home alone.

Lizzie met her at the gate
Full of wise upbraidings:
'Dear, you should not stay so late,

Twilight is not good for maidens;
Should not loiter in the glen
In the haunts of goblin men.
Do you not remember Jeanie,
How she met them in the moonlight,
Took their gifts both choice and many,
Ate their fruits and wore their flowers
Plucked from bowers
Where summer ripens at all hours?
But ever in the noonlight
She pined and pined away;
Sought them by night and day,
Found them no more but dwindled and grew
    grey;
Then fell with the first snow,
While to this day no grass will grow
Where she lies low:
I planted daisies there a year ago
That never blow.
You should not loiter so.'
'Nay, hush,' said Laura:
'Nay, hush, my sister:
I ate and ate my fill,
Yet my mouth waters still;
Tomorrow night I will
Buy more:' and kissed her:
'Have done with sorrow;
I'll bring you plums tomorrow

Fresh on their mother twigs,
Cherries worth getting;
You cannot think what figs
My teeth have met in,
What melons icy-cold
Piled on a dish of gold
Too huge for me to hold,
What peaches with a velvet nap,
Pellucid grapes without one seed:
Odorous indeed must be the mead
Whereon they grow, and pure the wave they drink
With lilies at the brink,
And sugar-sweet their sap.'

Golden head by golden head,
Like two pigeons in one nest
Folded in each other's wings,
They lay down in their curtained bed:
Like two blossoms on one stem,
Like two flakes of new-fall'n snow,
Like two wands of ivory
Tipped with gold for awful kings.
Moon and stars gazed in at them,
Wind sang to them lullaby,
Lumbering owls forbore to fly,
Not a bat flapped to and fro
Round their rest:
Cheek to cheek and breast to breast
Locked together in one nest.

Early in the morning
When the first cock crowed his warning,
Neat like bees, as sweet and busy,
Laura rose with Lizzie:
Fetched in honey, milked the cows,
Aired and set to rights the house,
Kneaded cakes of whitest wheat,
Cakes for dainty mouths to eat,
Next churned butter, whipped up cream,
Fed their poultry, sat and sewed;
Talked as modest maidens should:
Lizzie with an open heart,
Laura in an absent dream,
One content, one sick in part;
One warbling for the mere bright day's delight,
One longing for the night.

At length slow evening came:
They went with pitchers to the reedy brook;
Lizzie most placid in her look,
Laura most like a leaping flame.
They drew the gurgling water from its deep;
Lizzie plucked purple and rich golden flags,
Then turning homewards said: 'The sunset flushes
Those furthest loftiest crags;
Come, Laura, not another maiden lags,
No wilful squirrel wags,
The beasts and birds are fast asleep.'
But Laura loitered still among the rushes
And said the bank was steep.

And said the hour was early still,
The dew not fall'n, the wind not chill:
Listening ever, but not catching
The customary cry,
'Come buy, come buy,'
With its iterated jingle
Of sugar-baited words:
Not for all her watching
Once discerning even one goblin
Racing, whisking, tumbling, hobbling;
Let alone the herds
That used to tramp along the glen,
In groups or single,
Of brisk fruit-merchant men.
Till Lizzie urged, 'O Laura, come;
I hear the fruit-call but I dare not look:
You should not loiter longer at this brook:
Come with me home.
The stars rise, the moon bends her arc,
Each glowworm winks her spark,
Let us get home before the night grows dark:
For clouds may gather
Tho' this is summer weather,
Put out the lights and drench us thro';
Then if we lost our way what should we do?'

Laura turned cold as stone
To find her sister heard that cry alone,
That goblin cry,
'Come buy our fruits, come buy.'
Must she then buy no more such dainty fruit?

Must she no more such succous pasture find,
Gone deaf and blind?
Her tree of life drooped from the root:
She said not one word in her heart's sore ache;
But peering thro' the dimness, nought discerning,
Trudged home, her pitcher dripping all the way;
So crept to bed, and lay
Silent till Lizzie slept;
Then sat up in a passionate yearning,
And gnashed her teeth for baulked desire, and wept
As if her heart would break.

Day after day, night after night,
Laura kept watch in vain
In sullen silence of exceeding pain.
She never caught again the goblin cry:
'Come buy, come buy;'—
She never spied the goblin men
Hawking their fruits along the glen:
But when the noon waxed bright
Her hair grew thin and gray;
She dwindled, as the fair full moon doth turn
To swift decay and burn
Her fire away.

One day remembering her kernel-stone
She set it by a wall that faced the south;
Dewed it with tears, hoped for a root,
Watched for a waxing shoot,
But there came none;
It never saw the sun,

It never felt the trickling moisture run:
While with sunk eyes and faded mouth
She dreamed of melons, as a traveller sees
False waves in desert drouth
With shade of leaf-crowned trees,
And burns the thirstier in the sandful breeze.

She no more swept the house,
Tended the fowls or cows,
Fetched honey, kneaded cakes of wheat,
Brought water from the brook:
But sat down listless in the chimney-nook
And would not eat.

Tender Lizzie could not bear
To watch her sister's cankerous care
Yet not to share.
She night and morning
Caught the goblins' cry:
'Come buy our orchard fruits,
Come buy, come buy;'—
Beside the brook, along the glen,
She heard the tramp of goblin men,
The voice and stir
Poor Laura could not hear;
Longed to buy fruit to comfort her,
But feared to pay too dear.
She thought of Jeanie in her grave,
Who should have been a bride;
But who for joys brides hope to have
Fell sick and died

In her gay prime,
In earliest Winter time,
With the first glazing rime,
With the first snow-fall of crisp Winter time.

Till Laura dwindling
Seemed knocking at Death's door:
Then Lizzie weighed no more
Better and worse;
But put a silver penny in her purse,
Kissed Laura, crossed the heath with clumps
    of furze
At twilight, halted by the brook:
And for the first time in her life
Began to listen and look.

Laughed every goblin
When they spied her peeping:
Came towards her hobbling,
Flying, running, leaping,
Puffing and blowing,
Chuckling, clapping, crowing,
Clucking and gobbling,
Mopping and mowing,
Full of airs and graces,
Pulling wry faces,
Demure grimaces,
Cat-like and rat-like,
Ratel- and wombat-like,
Snail-paced in a hurry,
Parrot-voiced and whistler,

Helter skelter, hurry skurry,
Chattering like magpies,
Fluttering like pigeons,
Gliding like fishes,—
Hugged her and kissed her,
Squeezed and caressed her:
Stretched up their dishes,
Panniers, and plates:
'Look at our apples
Russet and dun,
Bob at our cherries,
Bite at our peaches,
Citrons and dates,
Grapes for the asking,
Pears red with basking
Out in the sun,
Plums on their twigs;
Pluck them and suck them,
Pomegranates, figs.'—

'Good folk,' said Lizzie,
Mindful of Jeanie:
'Give me much and many:'—
Held out her apron,
Tossed them her penny.
'Nay, take a seat with us,
Honour and eat with us,'
They answered grinning:
'Our feast is but beginning.
Night yet is early,
Warm and dew-pearly,

Wakeful and starry:
Such fruits as these
No man can carry;
Half their bloom would fly,
Half their dew would dry,
Half their flavour would pass by.
Sit down and feast with us,
Be welcome guest with us,
Cheer you and rest with us.'—
'Thank you,' said Lizzie: 'But one waits
At home alone for me:
So without further parleying,
If you will not sell me any
Of your fruits tho' much and many,
Give me back my silver penny
I tossed you for a fee.'—
They began to scratch their pates,
No longer wagging, purring,
But visibly demurring,
Grunting and snarling.
One called her proud,
Cross-grained, uncivil;
Their tones waxed loud,
Their looks were evil.
Lashing their tails
They trod and hustled her,
Elbowed and jostled her,
Clawed with their nails,
Barking, mewing, hissing, mocking,
Tore her gown and soiled her stocking,
Twitched her hair out by the roots,

Stamped upon her tender feet,
Held her hands and squeezed their fruits
Against her mouth to make her eat.

White and golden Lizzie stood,
Like a lily in a flood,—
Like a rock of blue-veined stone
Lashed by tides obstreperously,—
Like a beacon left alone
In a hoary roaring sea,
Sending up a golden fire,—
Like a fruit-crowned orange-tree
White with blossoms honey-sweet
Sore beset by wasp and bee,—

Like a royal virgin town
Topped with gilded dome and spire
Close beleaguered by a fleet
Mad to tug her standard down.

One may lead a horse to water,
Twenty cannot make him drink.
Tho' the goblins cuffed and caught her,
Coaxed and fought her,
Bullied and besought her,
Scratched her, pinched her black as ink,
Kicked and knocked her,
Mauled and mocked her,
Lizzie uttered not a word;
Would not open lip from lip
Lest they should cram a mouthful in:

But laughed in heart to feel the drip
Of juice that syrupped all her face,
And lodged in dimples of her chin,
And streaked her neck which quaked like
    curd.
At last the evil people
Worn out by her resistance
Flung back her penny, kicked their fruit
Along whichever road they took,
Not leaving root or stone or shoot;
Some writhed into the ground,
Some dived into the brook
With ring and ripple,
Some scudded on the gale without a sound,
Some vanished in the distance.

In a smart, ache, tingle,
Lizzie went her way;
Knew not was it night or day;
Sprang up the bank, tore thro' the furze,
Threaded copse and dingle,
And heard her penny jingle
Bouncing in her purse,
Its bounce was music to her ear.
She ran and ran
As if she feared some goblin man
Dogged her with gibe or curse
Or something worse:
But not one goblin skurried after,
Nor was she pricked by fear;
The kind heart made her windy-paced

That urged her home quite out of breath with
    haste
And inward laughter.

She cried 'Laura,' up the garden,
'Did you miss me?
Come and kiss me.
Never mind my bruises,
Hug me, kiss me, suck my juices
Squeezed from goblin fruits for you,
Goblin pulp and goblin dew.
Eat me, drink me, love me;
Laura, make much of me:
For your sake I have braved the glen
And had to do with goblin merchant men.'

Laura started from her chair,
Flung her arms up in the air,
Clutched her hair:
'Lizzie, Lizzie, have you tasted
For my sake the fruit forbidden?
Must your light like mine be hidden,
Your young life like mine be wasted,
Undone in mine undoing
And ruined in my ruin,
Thirsty, cankered, goblin-ridden?'—

She clung about her sister,
Kissed and kissed and kissed her:
Tears once again
Refreshed her shrunken eyes,

Dropping like rain
After long sultry drouth;
Shaking with aguish fear, and pain,
She kissed and kissed her with a hungry mouth.

Her lips began to scorch,
That juice was wormwood to her tongue,
She loathed the feast:
Writhing as one possessed she leaped and sung,
Rent all her robe, and wrung
Her hands in lamentable haste,
And beat her breast.
Her locks streamed like the torch
Borne by a racer at full speed,
Or like the mane of horses in their flight,
Or like an eagle when she stems the light
Straight toward the sun,
Or like a caged thing freed,
Or like a flying flag when armies run.

Swift fire spread thro' her veins, knocked at her heart,
Met the fire smouldering there
And overbore its lesser flame;
She gorged on bitterness without a name:
Ah! fool, to choose such part
Of soul-consuming care!
Sense failed in the mortal strife:

Like the watch-tower of a town
Which an earthquake shatters down,
Like a lightning-stricken mast,

Like a wind-uprooted tree
Spun about,
Like a foam-topped waterspout
Cast down headlong in the sea,
She fell at last;
Pleasure past and anguish past,
Is it death or is it life?

Life out of death.
That night long Lizzie watched by her,
Counted her pulse's flagging stir,
Felt for her breath,
Held water to her lips, and cooled her face
With tears and fanning leaves:
But when the first birds chirped about their eaves,
And early reapers plodded to the place
Of golden sheaves,
And dew-wet grass
Bowed in the morning winds so brisk to pass,
And new buds with new day
Opened of cup-like lilies on the stream,
Laura awoke as from a dream,
Laughed in the innocent old way,
Hugged Lizzie but not twice or thrice;
Her gleaming locks showed not one thread of grey,
Her breath was sweet as May
And light danced in her eyes.

Days, weeks, months, years
Afterwards, when both were wives
With children of their own;
Their mother-hearts beset with fears,
Their lives bound up in tender lives;
Laura would call the little ones
And tell them of her early prime,
Those pleasant days long gone
Of not-returning time:
Would talk about the haunted glen,
The wicked, quaint fruit-merchant men,
Their fruits like honey to the throat
But poison in the blood;
(Men sell not such in any town:)
Would tell them how her sister stood
In deadly peril to do her good,
And win the fiery antidote:
Then joining hands to little hands
Would bid them cling together,
'For there is no friend like a sister
In calm or stormy weather;
To cheer one on the tedious way,
To fetch one if one goes astray,
To lift one if one totters down,
To strengthen whilst one stands.'

The Queen of Hearts

How comes it, Flora, that, whenever we
Play cards together, you invariably,
    However the pack parts,
      Still hold the Queen of Hearts?

I've scanned you with a scrutinizing gaze,
Resolved to fathom these your secret ways:
    But, sift them as I will,
      Your ways are secret still.

I cut and shuffle; shuffle, cut, again;
But all my cutting, shuffling, proves in vain:
    Vain hope, vain forethought too;
      That Queen still falls to you.

I dropped her once, prepense; but, ere the deal
Was dealt, your instinct seemed her loss to feel:
    'There should be one card more,'
      You said, and searched the floor.

I cheated once; I made a private notch
In Heart-Queen's back, and kept a lynx-eyed watch;
    Yet such another back
      Deceived me in the pack:

The Queen of Clubs assumed by arts unknown
An imitative dint that seemed my own;
    This notch, not of my doing,
    Misled me to my ruin.

It baffles me to puzzle out the clue,
Which must be skill, or craft, or luck in you:
    Unless, indeed, it be
    Natural affinity.

Beauty Is Vain

While roses are so red,
    While lilies are so white,
Shall a woman exalt her face
    Because it gives delight?
She's not so sweet as a rose,
    A lily's straighter than she,
And if she were as red or white
    She'd be but one of three.

Whether she flush in love's summer
    Or in its winter grow pale,
Whether she flaunt her beauty
    Or hide it away in a veil,
Be she red or white,
    And stand she erect or bowed,
Time will win the race he runs with her
    And hide her away in a shroud.

A Birthday

My heart is like a singing bird
    Whose nest is in a watered shoot;
My heart is like an apple tree
    Whose boughs are bent with thickset fruit;
My heart is like a rainbow shell
    That paddles in a halcyon sea;
My heart is gladder than all these
    Because my love is come to me.

Raise me a dais of silk and down;
    Hang it with vair and purple dyes;
Carve it in doves and pomegranates,
    And peacocks with a hundred eyes;
Work it in gold and silver grapes,
    In leaves and silver fleurs-de-lys;
Because the birthday of my life
    Is come, my love is come to me.

Memory

1.

I nursed it in my bosom while it lived,
　　I hid it in my heart when it was dead;
In joy I sat alone, even so I grieved
　　　Alone and nothing said.

I shut the door to face the naked truth,
　　I stood alone—I faced the truth alone,
Stripped bare of self-regard or forms or ruth
　　　Till first and last were shown.

I took the perfect balances and weighed;
　　No shaking of my hand disturbed the poise;
Weighed, found it wanting: not a word I said,
　　　But silent made my choice.

None know the choice I made; I make it still.
　　None know the choice I made and broke my heart,
Breaking mine idol: I have braced my will
　　　Once, chosen for once my part.

I broke it at a blow, I laid it cold,
    Crushed in my deep heart where it used to live.
My heart dies inch by inch; the time grows old,
    Grows old in which I grieve.

II.

I have a room whereinto no one enters
    Save I myself alone:
    There sits a blessed memory on a throne,
There my life centres;

While winter comes and goes—oh tedious
        comer!—
    And while its nip-wind blows;
    While bloom the bloodless lily and warm rose
Of lavish summer.

If any should force entrance he might see there
    One buried yet not dead,
    Before whose face I no more bow my head
Or bend my knee there;

But often in my worn life's autumn weather
    I watch there with clear eyes,
    And think how it will be in Paradise
When we're together.

A Smile and a Sigh

A smile because the nights are short!
    And every morning brings such pleasure
Of sweet love-making, harmless sport:
    Love that makes and finds its treasure;
    Love, treasure without measure.

A sigh because the days are long!
    Long long these days that pass in sighing,
A burden saddens every song:
    While time lags which should be flying,
    We live who would be dying.

Autumn Violets

Keep love for youth, and violets for the spring:
    Or if these bloom when worn-out autumn grieves,
    Let them lie hid in double shade of leaves,
Their own, and others dropped down withering;
For violets suit when home birds build and sing,
    Not when the outbound bird a passage cleaves;
    Not with dry stubble of mown harvest sheaves,
But when the green world buds to blossoming.
Keep violets for the spring, and love for youth,
    Love that should dwell with beauty, mirth, and hope:
    Or if a later sadder love be born,
Let this not look for grace beyond its scope,
But give itself, nor plead for answering truth—
    A grateful Ruth tho' gleaning scanty corn.

'They Desire a Better Country'

I.

I would not if I could undo my past,
   Tho' for its sake my future is a blank;
   My past for which I have myself to thank,
For all its faults and follies first and last.
I would not cast anew the lot once cast,
   Or launch a second ship for one that sank,
   Or drug with sweets the bitterness I drank,
Or break by feasting my perpetual fast.
I would not if I could: for much more dear
   Is one rememberance than a hundred joys,
     More than a thousand hopes in jubilee;
   Dearer the music of one tearful voice
     That unforgotten calls and calls to me,
'Follow me here, rise up, and follow here.'

II.

   What seekest thou, far in the unknown land?
   In hope I follow joy gone on before;
   In hope and fear persistent more and more,
As the dry desert lengthens out its sand.
Whilst day and night I carry in my hand
   The golden key to ope the golden door
   Of golden home; yet mine eye weepeth sore,

For long the journey is that makes no stand.
And who is this that veiled doth walk with thee?
   Lo, this is Love that walketh at my right;
      One exile holds us both, and we are bound
   To selfsame home-joys in the land of light.
Weeping thou walkest with him; weepeth he?—
      Some sobbing weep, some weep and make no sound.

III.

A dimness of a glory glimmers here
   Thro' veils and distance from the space remote,
   A faintest far vibration of a note
Reaches to us and seems to bring us near;
Causing our face to glow with braver cheer,
   Making the serried mist to stand afloat,
   Subduing languor with an antidote,
And strengthening love almost to cast out fear:
Till for one moment golden city walls
   Rise looming on us, golden walls of home,
Light of our eyes until the darkness falls;
   Then thro' the outer darkness burdensome
I hear again the tender voice that calls,
   'Follow me hither, follow, rise, and come.'

Confluents

As rivers seek the sea,
 Much more deep than they,
So my soul seeks thee
 Far away:
As running rivers moan
On their course alone,
 So I moan
 Left alone.

As the delicate rose
 To the sun's sweet strength
Doth herself unclose,
 Breadth and length;
So spreads my heart to thee
Unveiled utterly,
 I to thee
 Utterly.

As morning dew exhales
 Sunwards pure and free,
So my spirit fails
 After thee:
As dew leaves not a trace
On the green earth's face;
 I, no trace
 On thy face.

Its goal the river knows,
   Dewdrops find a way,
Sunlight cheers the rose
   In her day:
Shall I, lone sorrow past,
Find thee at the last?
   Sorrow past,
     Thee at last?

'Hollow-sounding and Mysterious'

There's no replying
To the Wind's sighing,
Telling, foretelling,
Dying, undying,
Dwindling and swelling,
Complaining, droning,
Whistling and moaning,
Ever beginning,
Ending, repeating,
Hinting and dinning,
Lagging and fleeting—
We've no replying
Living or dying
To the Wind's sighing.
What are you telling,
Variable Wind-tone?
What would be teaching,
O sinking, swelling,
Desolate Wind-moan?
Ever for ever
Teaching and preaching,
Never, ah never
Making us wiser—
The earliest riser
Catches no meaning,
The last who hearkens

Garners no gleaning
Of wisdom's treasure,
While the world darkens:—
Living or dying,
In pain, in pleasure,
We've no replying
To wordless flying
Wind's sighing.

At Last

Many have sung of love a root of bane:
    While to my mind a root of balm it is,
    For love at length breeds love; sufficient bliss
For life and death and rising up again.
Surely when light of Heaven makes all things plain,
    Love will grow plain with all its mysteries;
    Nor shall we need to fetch from over seas
Wisdom or wealth or pleasure safe from pain.
Love in our borders, love within our heart,
    Love all in all, we then shall bide at rest,
    Ended for ever life's unending quest,
        Ended for ever effort, change and fear:
Love all in all;—no more that better part
    Purchased, but at the cost of all things here.

The Thread of Life

1.

The irresponsive silence of the land,
   The irresponsive sounding of the sea,
   Speak both one message of one sense to me:—
Aloof, aloof, we stand aloof, so stand
Thou too aloof bound with the flawless band
   Of inner solitude; we bind not thee;
   But who from thy self-chain shall set thee free?
What heart shall touch thy heart? what hand thy hand?—
And I am sometimes proud and sometimes meek,
   And sometimes I remember days of old
When fellowship seemed not so far to seek
   And all the world and I seemed much less cold,
   And at the rainbow's foot lay surely gold,
And hope felt strong and life itself not weak.

2.

Thus am I mine own prison. Everything
   Around me free and sunny and at ease:
   Or if in shadow, in a shade of trees
Which the sun kisses, where the gay birds sing
And where all winds make various murmuring;
   Where bees are found, with honey for the bees;

Where sounds are music, and where silences
Are music of an unlike fashioning.
Then gaze I at the merrymaking crew.
    And smile a moment and a moment sigh
Thinking: Why can I not rejoice with you?
    But soon I put the foolish fancy by:
I am not what I have nor what I do;
    But what I was I am, I am even I.

3.

Therefore myself is that one only thing
    I hold to use or waste, to keep or give;
    My sole possession every day I live,
And still mine own despite Time's winnowing.
Ever mine own, while moons and seasons bring
    From crudeness ripeness mellow and sanative;
    Ever mine own, till Death shall ply his sieve;
And still mine own, when saints break grave and sing.
And this myself as king unto my King
    I give, to Him Who gave Himself for me;
Who gives Himself to me, and bids me sing
    A sweet new song of His redeemed set free;
He bids me sing: O death, where is thy sting?
    And sing: O grave, where is thy victory?

Touching 'Never'

Because you never yet have loved me, dear,
    Think you you never can nor ever will?
    Surely while life remains hope lingers still,
Hope the last blossom of life's dying year.
Because the season and mine age grow sere,
    Shall never Spring bring forth her daffodil,
    Shall never sweeter Summer feast her fill
Of roses with the nightingales they hear?
If you had loved me, I not loving you,
    If you had urged me with the tender plea
Of what our unknown years to come might do
(Eternal years, if Time should count too few),
    I would have owned the point you pressed on me,
Was possible, or probable, or true.

An Old-World Thicket

... 'Una selva oscura.'—Dante.

Awake or sleeping (for I know not which)
   I was or was not mazed within a wood
   Where every mother-bird brought up her brood
      Safe in some leafy niche
   Of oak or ash, of cypress or of beech,

Of silvery aspen trembling delicately,
   Of plane or warmer-tinted sycamore,
   Of elm that dies in secret from the core,
      Of ivy weak and free,
   Of pines, of all green lofty things that be.

Such birds they seemed as challenged each desire;
   Like spots of azure heaven upon the wing,
   Like downy emeralds that alight and sing,
      Like actual coals on fire,
   Like anything they seemed, and everything.

Such mirth they made, such warblings and such chat
   With tongue of music in a well-tuned beak,
   They seemed to speak more wisdom than we speak,
      To make our music flat
   And all our subtlest reasonings wild or weak.

Their meat was nought but flowers like butterflies,
    With berries coral-coloured or like gold;
      Their drink was only dew, which blossoms hold
        Deep where the honey lies;
Their wings and tails were lit by sparkling eyes.

The shade wherein they revelled was a shade
    That danced and twinkled to the unseen sun;
      Branches and leaves cast shadows one by one,
        And all their shadows swayed
In breaths of air that rustled and that played.

A sound of waters neither rose nor sank,
    And spread a sense of freshness through the air;
      It seemed not here or there, but everywhere,
        As if the whole earth drank,
Root fathom deep and strawberry on its bank.

But I who saw such things as I have said,
    Was overdone with utter weariness;
      And walked in care, as one whom fears oppress
        Because above his head
Death hangs, or damage, or the dearth of bread.

Each sore defeat of my defeated life
    Faced and outfaced me in that bitter hour;
      And turned to yearning palsy all my power,
        And all my peace to strife,
Self stabbing self with keen lack-pity knife.

Sweetness of beauty moved me to despair,
    Stung me to anger by its mere content,
    Made me all lonely on that way I went,
        Piled care upon my care,
Brimmed full my cup, and stripped me empty and bare:

For all that was but showed what all was not,
    But gave clear proof of what might never be;
    Making more destitute my poverty,
        And yet more blank my lot,
And me much sadder by its jubilee.

Therefore I sat me down: for wherefore walk?
    And closed mine eyes: for wherefore see or hear?
    Alas, I had no shutter to mine ear,
        And could not shun the talk
Of all rejoicing creatures far or near.

Without my will I hearkened and I heard
    (Asleep or waking, for I know not which),
    Till note by note the music changed its pitch;
        Bird ceased to answer bird,
And every wind sighed softly if it stirred.

The drip of widening waters seemed to weep,
    All fountains sobbed and gurgled as they sprang,
Somewhere a cataract cried out in its leap
        Sheer down a headlong steep;
    High over all cloud-thunders gave a clang.

Such universal sound of lamentation
   I heard and felt, fain not to feel or hear;
   Nought else there seemed but anguish far and near;
      Nought else but all creation
   Moaning and groaning wrung by pain or fear,

Shuddering in the misery of its doom:
   My heart then rose a rebel against light,
   Scouring all earth and heaven and depth and height,
      Ingathering wrath and gloom,
Ingathering wrath to wrath and night to night.

Ah me, the bitterness of such revolt,
   All impotent, all hateful, and all hate,
That kicks and breaks itself against the bolt
      Of an imprisoning fate,
   And vainly shakes, and cannot shake the gate.

Agony to agony, deep called to deep,
   Out of the deep I called of my desire;
   My strength was weakness and my heart was fire;
      Mine eyes that would not weep
Or sleep, scaled height and depth, and could not sleep;

The eyes, I mean, of my rebellious soul,
   For still my bodily eyes were closed and dark:
   A random thing I seemed without a mark,
      Racing without a goal,
   Adrift upon life's sea without an ark.

More leaden than the actual self of lead
   Outer and inner darkness weighed on me.
   The tide of anger ebbed. Then fierce and free
      Surged full above my head
   The moaning tide of helpless misery.

Why should I breathe, whose breath was but a sigh?
   Why should I live, who drew such painful breath?
Oh weary work, the unanswerable why!—
      Yet I, why should I die,
   Who had no hope in life, no hope in death?

Grasses and mosses and the fallen leaf
   Make peaceful bed for an indefinite term;
   But underneath the grass there gnaws a worm—
      Haply, there gnaws a grief—
Both, haply always; not, as now, so brief.

The pleasure I remember, it is past;
   The pain I feel, is passing passing by;
   Thus all the world is passing, and thus I:
      All things that cannot last
   Have grown familiar, and are born to die.

And being familiar, have so long been borne
   That habit trains us not to break but bend:
Mourning grows natural to us who mourn
      In foresight of an end,
   But that which ends not who shall brave or mend?

Surely the ripe fruits tremble on their bough,
    They cling and linger trembling till they drop:
I, trembling, cling to dying life; for how
        Face the perpetual Now?
    Birthless, and deathless, void of start or stop,

Void of repentance, void of hope and fear,
    Of possibility, alternative,
    Of all that ever made us bear to live
        From night to morning here,
    Of promise even which has no gift to give.

The wood, and every creature of the wood,
    Seemed mourning with me in an undertone;
    Soft scattered chirpings and a windy moan,
        Trees rustling where they stood
And shivered, showed, compassion for my mood.

Rage to despair; and now despair had turned
    Back to self-pity and mere weariness,
With yearnings like a smouldering fire that burned,
        And might grow more or less,
    And might die out or wax to white excess.

Without, within me, music seemed to be;
    Something not music, yet most musical,
Silence and sound in heavenly harmony;
        At length a pattering fall
    Of feet, a bell, and bleatings, broke through all.

Then I looked up. The wood lay in a glow
    From golden sunset and from ruddy sky;
      The sun had stooped to earth though once so high;
        Had stooped to earth, in slow
Warm dying loveliness brought near and low.

Each water drop made answer to the light,
    Lit up a spark and showed the sun his face;
      Soft purple shadows paved the grassy space
        And crept from height to height,
From height to loftier height crept up apace.

While opposite the sun a gazing moon
    Put on his glory for her coronet,
Kindling her luminous coldness to its noon,
        As his great splendour set;
    One only star made up her train as yet.

Each twig was tipped with gold, each leaf was edged
    And veined with gold from the gold-flooded west;
Each mother-bird, and mate-bird, and unfledged
        Nestling, and curious nest,
    Displayed a gilded moss or beak or breast.

And filing peacefully between the trees,
    Having the moon behind them, and the sun
Full in their meek mild faces, walked at ease
        A homeward flock, at peace
    With one another and with every one.

A patriarchal ram with tinkling bell
    Led all his kin; sometimes one browsing sheep
    Hung back a moment, or one lamb would leap
        And frolic in a dell;
Yet still they kept together, journeying well,

And bleating, one or other, many or few,
    Journeying together toward the sunlit west;
    Mild face by face, and woolly breast by breast,
        Patient, sun-brightened too,
    Still journeying toward the sunset and their rest.

Another Spring

If I might see another Spring
   I'd not plant summer flowers and wait:
I'd have my crocuses at once,
My leafless pink mezereons,
   My chill-veined snowdrops, choicer yet
   My white or azure violet,
Leaf-nested primrose; anything
     To blow at once, not late.

If I might see another Spring
   I'd listen to the daylight birds
That build their nests and pair and sing,
Nor wait for mateless nightingale;
   I'd listen to the lusty herds,
   The ewes with lambs as white as snow,
I'd find out music in the hail
     And all the winds that blow.

If I might see another Spring—
   Oh stinging comment on my past
That all my past results in 'if'—
   If I might see another Spring
I'd laugh today, today is brief;
I would not wait for anything:
   I'd use today that cannot last,
     Be glad today and sing.

'Redeeming the Time'

A life of hope deferred too often is
A life of wasted opportunities;
A life of perished hope too often is
A life of all-lost opportunities:
Yet hope is but the flower and not the root,
And hope is still the flower and not the fruit;—
Arise and sow and weed: a day shall come
When also thou shalt keep thy harvest home.

A Castle-Builder's World

'The line of confusion, and the stones of emptiness.'

Unripe harvest there hath none to reap it
   From the misty gusty place,
Unripe vineyard there hath none to keep it
   In unprofitable space.
Living men and women are not found there,
   Only masks in flocks and shoals;
Flesh-and-bloodless hazy masks surround there,
   Ever wavering orbs and poles;
Flesh-and-bloodless vapid masks abound there,
   Shades of bodies without souls.

    Piteous my rhyme is
  What while I muse of love and pain,
  Of love misspent, of love in vain,
  Of love that is not loved again:
    And is this all then?
    As long as time is,
  Love loveth. Time is but a span,
  The dalliance space of dying man:
  And is this all immortals can?
    The gain were small then.

    Love loves for ever,
  And finds a sort of joy in pain,
  And gives with nought to take again,
  And loves too well to end in vain:
    Is the gain small then?
    Love laughs at 'never,'
Outlives our life, exceeds the span
Appointed to mere mortal man:
All which love is and does and can
    Is all in all then.

If love is not worth loving, then life is not worth living,
  Nor aught is worth remembering but well forgot;
For store is not worth storing and gifts are not worth
    giving,
  If love is not;

  And idly cold is death-cold, and life-heat idly hot,
And vain is any offering and vainer our receiving,
  And vanity of vanities is all our lot.
Better than life's heaving heart is death's heart
    unheaving,
  Better than the opening leaves are the leaves that rot,
For there is nothing left worth achieving or retrieving,
  If love is not.

    Roses on a brier,
      Pearls from out the bitter sea,
    Such is earth's desire
      However pure it be.

Neither bud nor brier,
    Neither pearl nor brine for me.
Be stilled, my long desire;
    There shall be no more sea.

Be stilled, my passionate heart;
    Old earth shall end, new earth shall be:
Be still, and earn thy part
    Where shall be no more sea.

Three Seasons

'A cup for hope!' she said,
In springtime ere the bloom was old:
The crimson wine was poor and cold
    By her mouth's richer red.

'A cup for love!' how low,
How soft the words; and all the while
Her blush was rippling with a smile
    Like summer after snow.

'A cup for memory!'
Cold cup that one must drain alone:
While autumn winds are up and moan
    Across the barren sea.

Hope, memory, love:
Hope for fair morn, and love for day,
And memory for the evening grey
    And solitary dove.

One Day

I will tell you when they met:
In the limpid days of Spring;
Elder boughs were budding yet,
Oaken boughs looked wintry still,
But primrose and veined violet
In the mossful turf were set,
While meeting birds made haste to sing
And build with right good will.

I will tell you when they parted:
When plenteous Autumn sheaves were brown,
Then they parted heavy-hearted;
The full rejoicing sun looked down
As grand as in the days before;
Only they had lost a crown:
Only to them those days of yore
Could come back nevermore.

When shall they meet? I cannot tell,
Indeed, when they shall meet again,
Except some day in Paradise:
For this they wait, one waits in pain.
Beyond the sea of death love lies
For ever, yesterday, today;
Angels shall ask them, 'Is it well?'
And they shall answer, 'Yea.'

An Apple Gathering

I plucked pink blossoms from mine apple-tree
    And wore them all that evening in my hair:
Then in due season when I went to see
    I found no apples there.

With dangling basket all along the grass
    As I had come I went the selfsame track:
My neighbours mocked me while they saw me pass
    So empty-handed back.

Lilian and Lilias smiled in trudging by,
    Their heaped-up basket teased me like a jeer;
Sweet-voiced they sang beneath the sunset sky,
    Their mother's home was near.

Plump Gertrude passed me with her basket full,
    A stronger hand than hers helped it along;
A voice talked with her through the shadows cool
    More sweet to me than song.

Ah Willie, Willie, was my love less worth
    Than apples with their green leaves piled above?
I counted rosiest apples on the earth
    Of far less worth than love.

So once it was with me you stooped to talk
    Laughing and listening in this very lane:
To think that by this way we used to walk
    We shall not walk again!

I let me neighbours pass me, ones and twos
    And groups; the latest said the night grew chill,
And hastened: but I loitered, while the dews
    Fell fast I loitered still.

Grown and Flown

I loved my love from green of Spring
    Until sere Autumn's fall;
But now that leaves are withering
    How should one love at all?
    One heart's too small
For hunger, cold, love, everything.

I loved my love on sunny days
    Until late Summer's wane;
But now that frost begins to glaze
    How should one love again?
    Nay, love and pain
Walk wide apart in diverse ways.

I loved my love—alas to see
    That this should be, alas!
I thought that this could scarcely be,
    Yet has it come to pass:
    Sweet sweet love was,
Now bitter bitter grown to me.

A Farm Walk

The year stood at its equinox
    And bluff the North was blowing,
A bleat of lambs came from the flocks,
    Green hardy things were growing;
I met a maid with shining locks
    Where milky kine were lowing.

She wore a kerchief on her neck,
    Her bare arm showed its dimple,
Her apron spread without a speck,
    Her air was frank and simple.

She milked into a wooden pail
    And sang a country ditty,
An innocent fond lovers' tale,
    That was not wise nor witty,
Pathetically rustical,
    Too pointless for the city.

She kept in time without a beat
    As true as church-bell ringers,
Unless she tapped time with her feet,
    Or squeezed it with her fingers;
Her clear unstudied notes were sweet
    As many a practised singer's.

I stood a minute out of sight,
    Stood silent for a minute
To eye the pail, and creamy white
    The frothing milk within it;

To eye the comely milking maid
    Herself so fresh and creamy:
'Good day to you,' at last I said;
    She turned her head to see me:
'Good day,' she said with lifted head;
    Her eyes looked soft and dreamy,

And all the while she milked and milked
    The grave cow heavy-laden:
I've seen grand ladies plumed and silked,
    But not a sweeter maiden;

But not a sweeter fresher maid
    Than this in homely cotton,
Whose pleasant face and silky braid
    I have not yet forgotten.

Seven springs have passed since then, as I
    Count with a sober sorrow;
Seven springs have come and passed me by,
    And spring sets in to-morrow.

I've half a mind to shake myself
    Free just for once from London,
To set my work upon the shelf
    And leave it done or undone;

To run down by the early train,
    Whirl down with shriek and whistle,
And feel the bluff North blow again,
    And mark the sprouting thistle
Set up on waste patch of the lane
    Its green and tender bristle.

And spy the scarce-blown violet banks,
    Crisp primrose leaves and others,
And watch the lambs leap at their pranks
    And butt their patient mothers.

Alas, one point in all my plan
    My serious thoughts demur to:
Seven years have passed for maid and man,
    Seven years have passed for her too;

Perhaps my rose is overblown,
    Not rosy or too rosy;
Perhaps in farmhouse of her own
    Some husband keeps her cosy,
Where I should show a face unknown.
    Good-bye, my wayside posy.

Somewhere or Other

Somewhere or other there must surely be
    The face not seen, the voice not heard,
The heart that not yet—never yet—ah me!
    Made answer to my word.

Somewhere or other, may be near or far;
    Past land and sea, clean out of sight;
Beyond the wandering moon, beyond the star
    That tracks her night by night.

Somewhere or other, may be far or near;
    With just a wall, a hedge, between;
With just the last leaves of the dying year
    Fallen on a turf grown green.

'The Iniquity of the Fathers upon the Children'

Oh the rose of keenest thorn!
One hidden summer morn
Under the rose I was born.

I do not guess his name
Who wrought my Mother's shame,
And gave me life forlorn,
But my Mother, Mother, Mother,
I know her from all other.
My Mother pale and mild,
Fair as ever was seen,
She was but scarce sixteen,
Little more than a child,
When I was born
To work her scorn.
With secret bitter throes,
In a passion of secret woes,
She bore me under the rose.

One who my Mother nursed
Took me from the first:—
'O nurse, let me look upon
This babe that costs so dear;
Tomorrow she will be gone:
Other mothers may keep

Their babes awake and asleep,
But I must not keep her here.'—
Whether I know or guess,
I know this not the less.

So I was sent away
That none might spy the truth:
And my childhood waxed to youth
And I left off childish play.
I never cared to play
With the village boys and girls;
And I think they thought me proud,
I found so little to say
And kept so from the crowd:
But I had the longest curls
And I had the largest eyes,
And my teeth were small like pearls;
The girls might flout and scout me,
But the boys would hang about me
In sheepish mooning wise.

Our one-street village stood
A long mile from the town,
A mile of windy down
And bleak one-sided wood,
With not a single house.
Our town itself was small,
With just the common shops,
And throve in its small way.
Our neighbouring gentry reared
The good old-fashioned crops,

And made old-fashioned boasts
Of what John Bull would do
If Frenchman Frog appeared,
And drank old-fashioned toasts,
And made old-fashioned bows
To my Lady at the Hall.

My Lady at the Hall
Is grander than they all:
Hers is the oldest name
In all the neighbourhood;
But the race must die with her
Tho' she's a lofty dame,
For she's unmarried still.
Poor people say she's good
And has an open hand
As any in the land,
And she's the comforter
Of many sick and sad;
My nurse once said to me
That everything she had
Came of my Lady's bounty:
'Tho' she's greatest in the county
She's humble to the poor,
No beggar seeks her door
But finds help presently.
I pray both night and day
For her, and you must pray:
But she'll never feel distress
If needy folk can bless.'

I was a little maid
When here we came to live
From somewhere by the sea.
Men spoke a foreign tongue
There where we used to be
When I was merry and young,
Too young to feel afraid;
The fisher-folk would give
A kind strange word to me,
There by the foreign sea:
I don't know where it was,
But I remember still
Our cottage on a hill,
And fields of flowering grass
On that fair foreign shore.

I liked my old home best,
But this was pleasant too:
So here we made our nest
And here I grew.
And now and then my Lady
In riding past our door
Would nod to Nurse and speak,
Or stoop and pat my cheek;
And I was always ready
To hold the field-gate wide
For my Lady to go thro';
My Lady in her veil
So seldom put aside,
My Lady grave and pale.

I often sat to wonder
Who might my parents be,
For I knew of something under
My simple-seeming state.
Nurse never talked to me
Of mother or of father,
But watched me early and late
With kind suspicious cares:
Or not suspicious, rather
Anxious, as if she knew
Some secret I might gather
And smart for unawares.
Thus I grew.

But Nurse waxed old and grey,
Bent and weak with years.
There came a certain day
That she lay upon her bed
Shaking her palsied head,
With words she gasped to say
Which had to stay unsaid.
Then with a jerking hand
Held out so piteously
She gave a ring to me
Of gold wrought curiously,
A ring which she had worn
Since the day that I was born,
She once had said to me:
I slipped it on my finger;
Her eyes were keen to linger
On my hand that slipped it on;

Then she sighed one rattling sigh
And stared on with sightless eyes:—
The one who loved me was gone.

How long I stayed alone
With the corpse, I never knew,
For I fainted dead as stone:
When I came to life once more
I was down upon the floor,
With neighbours making ado
To bring me back to life.
I heard the sexton's wife
Say: 'Up, my lad, and run
To tell it at the Hall;
She was my Lady's nurse,
And done can't be undone.
I'll watch by this poor lamb.
I guess my Lady's purse
Is always open to such:
I'd run up on my crutch
A cripple as I am,'
(For cramps had vexed her much)
'Rather than this dear heart
Lack one to take her part.'

For days day after day
On my weary bed I lay
Wishing the time would pass;
Oh, so wishing that I was
Likely to pass away:
For the one friend whom I knew

Was dead, I knew no other,
Neither father nor mother;
And I, what should I do?

One day the sexton's wife
Said: 'Rouse yourself, my dear:
My Lady has driven down
From the Hall into the town,
And we think she's coming here.
Cheer up, for life is life.'

But I would not look or speak,
Would not cheer up at all.
My tears were like to fall,
So I turned round to the wall
And hid my hollow cheek
Making as if I slept,
As silent as a stone,
And no one knew I wept.
What was my Lady to me,
The grand lady from the Hall?
She might come, or stay away,
I was sick at heart that day:
The whole world seemed to be
Nothing, just nothing to me,
For aught that I could see.

Yet I listened where I lay:
A bustle came below,
A clear voice said: 'I know;
I will see her first alone,
It may be less of a shock

If she's so weak today:'—
A light hand turned the lock,
A light step crossed the floor,
One sat beside my bed:
But never a word she said.

For me, my shyness grew
Each moment more and more:
So I said never a word
And neither looked nor stirred;
I think she must have heard
My heart go pit-a-pat:
Thus I lay, my Lady sat,
More than a mortal hour—
(I counted one and two
By the house-clock while I lay):
I seemed to have no power
To think of a thing to say,
Or do what I ought to do,
Or rouse myself to a choice.

At last she said: 'Margaret,
Won't you even look at me?'
A something in her voice
Forced my tears to fall at last,
Forced sobs from me thick and fast;
Something not of the past,
Yet stirring memory;
A something new, and yet
Not new, too sweet to last,
Which I never can forget.

I turned and stared at her:
Her cheek showed hollow-pale;
Her hair like mine was fair,
A wonderful fall of hair
That screened her like a veil;
But her height was statelier,
Her eyes had depth more deep;
I think they must have had
Always a something sad,
Unless they were asleep.

While I stared, my Lady took
My hand in her spare hand
Jewelled and soft and grand,
And looked with a long long look
Of hunger in my face;
As if she tried to trace
Features she ought to know,
And half hoped, half feared, to find.
Whatever was in her mind
She heaved a sigh at last,
And began to talk to me.

'Your nurse was my dear nurse,
And her nursling's dear,' said she:
'No one told me a word
Of her getting worse and worse,
Till her poor life was past'
(Here my Lady's tears dropped fast):
'I might have been with her,
I might have promised and heard,

But she had no comforter.
She might have told me much
Which now I shall never know,
Never never shall know.'
She sat by me sobbing so,
And seemed so woe-begone,
That I laid one hand upon
Hers with a timid touch,
Scarce thinking what I did,
Not knowing what to say:
That moment her face was hid
In the pillow close by mine,
Her arm was flung over me,
She hugged me, sobbing so
As if her heart would break,
And kissed me where I lay.

After this she often came
To bring me fruit or wine,
Or sometimes hothouse flowers.
And at nights I lay awake
Often and often thinking
What to do for her sake.
Wet or dry it was the same:
She would come in at all hours,
Set me eating and drinking
And say I must grow strong;
At last the day seemed long
And home seemed scarcely home
If she did not come.

Well, I grew strong again:
In time of primroses,
I went to pluck them in the lane;
In time of nestling birds,
I heard them chirping round the house;
And all the herds
Were out at grass when I grew strong,
And days were waxen long,
And there was work for bees
Among the May-bush boughs,
And I had shot up tall,
And life felt after all
Pleasant, and not so long
When I grew strong.

I was going to the Hall
To be my Lady's maid:
'Her little friend,' she said to me,
'Almost her child,'
She said and smiled
Sighing painfully;
Blushing, with a second flush
As if she blushed to blush.
Friend, servant, child: just this
My standing at the Hall;
The other servants call me 'Miss,'
My Lady calls me 'Margaret,'
With her clear voice musical.
She never chides when I forget
This or that; she never chides.
Except when people come to stay,

(And that's not often) at the Hall,
I sit with her all day
And ride out when she rides.
She sings to me and makes me sing;
Sometimes I read to her,
Sometimes we merely sit and talk.
She noticed once my ring
And made me tell its history:
That evening in our garden walk
She said she should infer
The ring had been my father's first,
Then my mother's, given for me
To the nurse who nursed
My mother in her misery,
That so quite certainly
Some one might know me, who . . .
Then she was silent, and I too.

I hate when people come:
The women speak and stare
And mean to be so civil.
This one will stroke my hair,
That one will pat my cheek
And praise my Lady's kindness,
Expecting me to speak;
I like the proud ones best
Who sit as struck with blindness,

As if I wasn't there.
But if any gentleman
Is staying at the Hall

(Tho' few come prying here),
My Lady seems to fear
Some downright dreadful evil,
And makes me keep my room
As closely as she can:
So I hate when people come,
It is so troublesome.
In spite of all her care,
Sometimes to keep alive
I sometimes do contrive
To get out in the grounds
For a whiff of wholesome air,
Under the rose you know:
It's charming to break bounds,
Stolen waters are sweet,
And what's the good of feet
If for days they mustn't go?
Give me a longer tether,
Or I may break from it.

Now I have eyes and ears
And just some little wit:
'Almost my Lady's child;'
I recollect she smiled,
Sighed and blushed together;
Then her story of the ring
Sounds not improbable,
She told it me so well
It seemed the actual thing:—
Oh, keep your counsel close,
But I guess under the rose,

In long past summer weather
When the world was blossoming,

And the rose upon its thorn:
I guess not who he was
Flawed honour like a glass
And made my life forlorn,
But my Mother, Mother, Mother,
Oh, I know her from all other.

My Lady, you might trust
Your daughter with your fame.
Trust me, I would not shame
Our honourable name,
For I have noble blood
Tho' I was bred in dust
And brought up in the mud.
I will not press my claim,
Just leave me where you will:
But you might trust your daughter,
For blood is thicker than water
And you're my mother still.

So my Lady holds her own
With condescending grace,
And fills her lofty place
With an untroubled face
As a queen may fill a throne.
While I could hint a tale—
(But then I am her child)—
Would make her quail;

Would set her in the dust,
Lorn with no comforter,
Her glorious hair defiled
And ashes on her cheek:
The decent world would thrust
Its finger out at her,
Not much displeased I think
To make a nine days' stir;
The decent world would sink
Its voice to speak of her.
Now this is what I mean
To do, no more, no less:
Never to speak, or show
Bare sign of what I know.
Let the blot pass unseen;
Yea, let her never guess
I hold the tangled clue
She huddles out of view.
Friend, servant, almost child,
So be it and nothing more
On this side of the grave.
Mother, in Paradise,
You'll see with clearer eyes;
Perhaps in this world even
When you are like to die
And face to face with Heaven
You'll drop for once the lie:
But you must drop the mask, not I.

My Lady promises
Two hundred pounds with me
Whenever I may wed
A man she can approve:
And since besides her bounty
I'm fairest in the county
(For so I've heard it said,
Tho' I don't vouch for this),
Her promised pounds may move
Some honest man to see
My virtues and my beauties;
Perhaps the rising grazier,
Or temperance publican,
May claim my wifely duties.
Meanwhile I wait their leisure
And grace-bestowing pleasure,
I wait the happy man;
But if I hold my head
And pitch my expectations
Just higher than their level,
They must fall back on patience:
I may not mean to wed,
Yet I'll be civil.

Now sometimes in a dream
My heart goes out of me
To build and scheme,
Till I sob after things that seem
So pleasant in a dream:
A home such as I see
My blessed neighbours live in

With father and with mother,
All proud of one another,
Named by one common name
From baby in the bud
To full-blown workman father;
It's little short of Heaven.
I'd give my gentle blood
To wash my special shame
And drown my private grudge;
I'd toil and moil much rather
The dingiest cottage drudge
Whose mother need not blush,
Than live here like a lady
And see my Mother flush
And hear her voice unsteady
Sometimes, yet never dare
Ask to share her care.

Of course the servants sneer
Behind my back at me;
Of course the village girls,
Who envy me my curls
And gowns and idleness,
Take comfort in a jeer;

Of course the ladies guess
Just so much of my history
As points the emphatic stress
With which they laud my Lady;
The gentlemen who catch
A casual glimpse of me

And turn again to see,
Their valets on the watch
To speak a word with me,
All know and sting me wild;
Till I am almost ready
To wish that I were dead,
No faces more to see,
No more words to be said,
My Mother safe at last
Disburdened of her child,
And the past past.

'All equal before God'—
Our Rector has it so,
And sundry sleepers nod:
It may be so; I know
All are not equal here,
And when the sleepers wake
They make a difference.
'All equal in the grave'—
That shows an obvious sense:
Yet something which I crave
Not death itself brings near;
How should death half atone
For all my past; or make
The name I bear my own?

I love my dear old Nurse
Who loved me without gains;
I love my mistress even,
Friend, Mother, what you will:

But I could almost curse
My Father for his pains;
And sometimes at my prayer
Kneeling in sight of Heaven
I almost curse him still:
Why did he set his snare
To catch at unaware
My Mother's foolish youth;
Load me with shame that's hers,
And her with something worse,
A lifelong lie for truth?

I think my mind is fixed
On one point and made up:
To accept my lot unmixed;
Never to drug the cup
But drink it by myself.
I'll not be wooed for pelf;
I'll not blot out my shame
With any man's good name;
But nameless as I stand,
My hand is my own hand,
And nameless as I came
I go to the dark land.

'All equal in the grave'—
I bide my time till then:
'All equal before God'—
Today I feel His rod,
Tomorrow He may save:
        Amen.

Love Lies Bleeding

Love that is dead and buried, yesterday
   Out of his grave rose up before my face,
   No recognition in his look, no trace
Of memory in his eyes dust-dimmed and grey.
While I, remembering, found no word to say,
   But felt my quickened heart leap in its place;
   Caught afterglow thrown back from long set days,
Caught echoes of all music passed away.
Was this indeed to meet? – I mind me yet
   In youth we met when hope and love were quick,
      We parted with hope dead, but love alive:
   I mind me how we parted then heart sick,
      Remembering, loving, hopeless, weak to strive:–
Was this to meet? Not so, we have not met.

A Bird's Song

It's a year almost that I have not seen her:
Oh, last summer green things were greener,
Brambles fewer, the blue sky bluer.

It's surely summer, for there's a swallow:
Come one swallow, his mate will follow,
The bird race quicken and wheel and thicken.

Oh happy swallow whose mate will follow
O'er height, o'er hollow! I'd be a swallow,
To build this weather one nest together.

Bird Raptures

The sunrise wakes the lark to sing,
  The moonrise wakes the nightingale.
Come darkness, moonrise, every thing
  That is so silent, sweet, and pale:
  Come, so ye wake the nightingale.

Make haste to mount, thou wistful moon,
  Make haste to wake the nightingale:
Let silence set the world in tune
  To hearken to that wordless tale
  Which warbles from the nightingale

O herald skylark, stay thy flight
  One moment, for a nightingale
Floods us with sorrow and delight.
  To-morrow thou shalt hoist the sail;
Leave us to-night the nightingale.

The Key-Note

Where are the songs I used to know,
    Where are the notes I used to sing?
    I have forgotten everything
I used to know so long ago;
Summer has followed after Spring;
    Now Autumn is so shrunk and sere,
I scarcely think a sadder thing
    Can be the Winter of my year.

Yet Robin sings thro' Winter's rest,
    When bushes put their berries on;
    While they their ruddy jewels don,
He sings out of a ruddy breast;
The hips and haws and ruddy breast
    Make one spot warm where snowflakes lie,
They break and cheer the unlovely rest
    Of Winter's pause—and why not I?

Winter Rain

Every valley drinks,
 Every dell and hollow:
Where the kind rain sinks and sinks,
 Green of Spring will follow.

Yet a lapse of weeks
 Buds will burst their edges,
Strip their wool-coats, glue-coats, streaks,
 In the woods and hedges;

Weave a bower of love
 For birds to meet each other,
Weave a canopy above
 Nest and egg and mother.

But for fattening rain
 We should have no flowers,
Never a bud or leaf again
 But for soaking showers;

Never a mated bird
 In the rocking tree-tops,
Never indeed a flock or herd
 To graze upon the lea-crops.

Lambs so woolly white,
   Sheep the sun-bright leas on,
They could have no grass to bite
   But for rain in season.

We should find no moss
   In the shadiest places,
Find no waving meadow grass
   Pied with broad-eyed daisies:

But miles of barren sand,
   With never a son or daughter,
Not a lily on the land,
   Or lily on the water.

The Lowest Room

Like flowers sequestered from the sun
    And wind of summer, day by day
I dwindled paler, whilst my hair
    Showed the first tinge of grey.

'Oh what is life, that we should live?
    Or what is death, that we must die?
A bursting bubble is our life:
    I also, what am I?'

'What is your grief? now tell me, sweet,
    That I may grieve,' my sister said;
And stayed a white embroidering hand
    And raised a golden head:

Her tresses showed a richer mass,
    Her eyes looked softer than my own,
Her figure had a statelier height,
    Her voice a tenderer tone.

'Some must be second and not first;
    All cannot be the first of all:
Is not this, too, but vanity?
    I stumble like to fall.

'So yesterday I read the acts
   Of Hector and each clangorous king
With wrathful great Aeacides:—
      Old Homer leaves a sting.'

The comely face looked up again,
   The deft hand lingered on the thread:
'Sweet, tell me what is Homer's sting,
      Old Homer's sting?' she said.

'He stirs my sluggish pulse like wine,
   He melts me like the wind of spice,
Strong as strong Ajax' red right hand,
      And grand like Juno's eyes.

'I cannot melt the sons of men,
   I cannot fire and tempest-toss:—
Besides, those days were golden days,
      Whilst these are days of dross.'

She laughed a feminine low laugh,
   Yet did not stay her dexterous hand:
'Now tell me of those days,' she said,
      'When time ran golden sand.'

'Then men were men of might and right,
   Sheer might, at least, and weighty swords;
Then men in open blood and fire
      Bore witness to their words,

'Crest-rearing kings with whistling spears;
    But if these shivered in the shock
They wrenched up hundred-rooted trees,
    Or hurled the effacing rock.

'Then hand to hand, then foot to foot,
    Stern to the death-grip grappling then,
Who ever thought of gunpowder
    Amongst these men of men?

'They knew whose hand struck home the death,
    They knew who broke but would not bend,
Could venerate an equal foe
    And scorn a laggard friend.

'Calm in the utmost stress of doom,
    Devout toward adverse powers above,
They hated with intenser hate
    And loved with fuller love.

'Then heavenly beauty could allay
    As heavenly beauty stirred the strife:
By them a slave was worshipped more
    Than is by us a wife.'

She laughed again, my sister laughed;
    Made answer o'er the laboured cloth:
'I rather would be one of us
    Than wife, or slave, or both.'

'Oh better then be slave or wife
   Than fritter now blank life away:
Then night had holiness of night,
    And day was sacred day.

'The princess laboured at her loom,
   Mistress and handmaiden alike;
Beneath their needles grew the field
    With warriors armed to strike.

'Or, look again, dim Dian's face
   Gleamed perfect thro' the attendant night;
Were such not better than those holes
    Amid that waste of white?

'A shame it is, our aimless life:
   I rather from my heart would feed
From silver dish in gilded stall
    With wheat and wine the steed—

'The faithful steed that bore my lord
   In safety thro' the hostile land,
The faithful steed that arched his neck
    To fondle with my hand.'

Her needle erred; a moment's pause,
   A moment's patience, all was well.
Then she: 'But just suppose the horse,
    Suppose the rider fell?

'Then captive in an alien house,
    Hungering on exile's bitter bread,—
They happy, they who won the lot
    Of sacrifice,' she said.

Speaking she faltered, while her look
    Showed forth her passion like a glass:
With hand suspended, kindling eye,
    Flushed cheek, how fair she was!

'Ah well, be those the days of dross;
    This, if you will, the age of gold:
Yet had those days a spark of warmth,
    While these are somewhat cold—

'Are somewhat mean and cold and slow,
    Are stunted from heroic growth:
We gain but little when we prove
    The worthlessness of both.'

'But life is in our hands,' she said:
    'In our own hands for gain or loss:
Shall not the Sevenfold Sacred Fire
    Suffice to purge our dross?

'Too short a century of dreams,
    One day of work sufficient length:
Why should not you, why should not I
    Attain heroic strength?

'Our life is given us as a blank;
   Ourselves must make it blest or curst:
Who dooms me I shall only be
    The second, not the first?

'Learn from old Homer, if you will,
   Such wisdom as his books have said:
In one the acts of Ajax shine,
    In one of Diomed.

'Honoured all heroes whose high deeds
   Thro' life, thro' death, enlarge their span:
Only Achilles in his rage
    And sloth is less than man.'

'Achilles only less than man?
   He less than man who, half a god,
Discomfited all Greece with rest,
    Cowed Ilion with a nod?

'He offered vengeance, lifelong grief
   To one dear ghost, uncounted price:
Beasts, Trojans, adverse gods, himself,
    Heaped up the sacrifice.

'Self-immolated to his friend,
   Shrined in world's wonder, Homer's page,
Is this the man, the less than men
    Of this degenerate age?'

'Gross from his acorns, tusky boar
    Does memorable acts like his;
So for her snared offended young
    Bleeds the swart lioness.'

But here she paused; our eyes had met,
    And I was whitening with the jeer;
She rose: 'I went too far,' she said;
    Spoke low: 'Forgive me, dear.

'To me our days seem pleasant days,
    Our home a haven of pure content;
Forgive me if I said too much,
    So much more than I meant.

'Homer, tho' greater than his gods,
    With rough-hewn virtues was sufficed
And rough-hewn men: but what are such
    To us who learn of Christ?'

The much-moved pathos of her voice,
    Her almost tearful eyes, her cheek
Grown pale, confessed the strength of love
    Which only made her speak:

For mild she was, of few soft words,
    Most gentle, easy to be led,
Content to listen when I spoke
    And reverence what I said;

I elder sister by six years;
    Not half so glad, or wise, or good:
Her words rebuked my secret self
        And shamed me where I stood.

She never guessed her words reproved
    A silent envy nursed within,
A selfish, souring discontent
        Pride-born, the devil's sin.

I smiled, half bitter, half in jest:
    'The wisest man of all the wise
Left for his summary of life
        'Vanity of vanities.'

'Beneath the sun there's nothing new:
    Men flow, men ebb, mankind flows on:
If I am wearied of my life,
        Why so was Solomon.

'Vanity of vanities he preached
    Of all he found, of all he sought:
Vanity of vanities, the gist
        Of all the words he taught.

'This in the wisdom of the world,
    In Homer's page, in all, we find:
As the sea is not filled, so yearns
        Man's universal mind.

'This Homer felt, who gave his men
   With glory but a transient state:
His very Jove could not reverse
   Irrevocable fate.

'Uncertain all their lot save this—
   Who wins must lose, who lives must die:
All trodden out into the dark
   Alike, all vanity.'

She scarcely answered when I paused,
   But rather to herself said: 'One
Is here,' low-voiced and loving, 'Yea,
   Greater than Solomon.'

So both were silent, she and I:
   She laid her work aside, and went
Into the garden-walks, like spring,
   All gracious with content;

A little graver than her wont,
   Because her words had fretted me;
Not warbling quite her merriest tune
   Bird-like from tree to tree.

I chose a book to read and dream:
   Yet half the while with furtive eyes
Marked how she made her choice of flowers
   Intuitively wise,

And ranged them with instinctive taste
    Which all my books had failed to teach;
Fresh rose herself, and daintier
    Than blossom of the peach.

By birthright higher than myself,
    Tho' nestling of the selfsame nest:
No fault of hers, no fault of mine,
    But stubborn to digest.

I watched her, till my book unmarked
    Slid noiseless to the velvet floor;
Till all the opulent summer-world
    Looked poorer than before.

Just then her busy fingers ceased,
    Her fluttered colour went and came;
I knew whose step was on the walk,
    Whose voice would name her name.

* * *

Well, twenty years have passed since then:
    My sister now, a stately wife
Still fair, looks back in peace and sees
    The longer half of life—

The longer half of prosperous life,
    With little grief, or fear, or fret:
She, loved and loving long ago,
    Is loved and loving yet.

A husband honourable, brave,
  Is her main wealth in all the world:
And next to him one like herself,
    One daughter golden-curled;

Fair image of her own fair youth,
  As beautiful and as serene,
With almost such another love
    As her own love has been.

Yet, tho' of world-wide charity,
  And in her home most tender dove,
Her treasure and her heart are stored
    In the home-land of love:

She thrives, God's blessed husbandry;
  Most like a vine which full of fruit
Doth cling and lean and climb toward heaven
    While earth still binds its root.

I sit and watch my sister's face:
  How little altered since the hours
When she, a kind, light-hearted girl,
    Gathered her garden flowers;

Her song just mellowed by regret
  For having teased me with her talk;
Then all-forgetful as she heard
    One step upon the walk.

While I? I sat alone and watched;
   My lot in life, to live alone
In mine own world of interests,
      Much felt but little shown.

Not to be first: how hard to learn
   That lifelong lesson of the past;
Line graven on line and stroke on stroke;
      But, thank God, learned at last.

So now in patience I possess
   My soul year after tedious year,
Content to take the lowest place,
      The place assigned me here.

Yet sometimes, when I feel my strength
   Most weak, and life most burdensome,
I lift mine eyes up to the hills
      From whence my help shall come:

Yea, sometimes still I lift my heart
   To the Archangelic trumpet-burst,
When all deep secrets shall be shown,
      And many last be first.

My Dream

Hear now a curious dream I dreamed last night,
Each word whereof is weighed and sifted truth.

I stood beside Euphrates while it swelled
Like overflowing Jordan in its youth:
It waxed and coloured sensibly to sight,
Till out of myriad pregnant waves there welled
Young crocodiles, a gaunt blunt-featured crew,
Fresh-hatched perhaps and daubed with birthday dew.
The rest if I should tell, I fear my friend,
My closest friend would deem the facts untrue;
And therefore it were wisely left untold;
Yet if you will, why, hear it to the end.

Each crocodile was girt with massive gold
And polished stones that with their wearers grew:
But one there was who waxed beyond the rest,
Wore kinglier girdle and a kingly crown,
Whilst crowns and orbs and sceptres starred his breast.
All gleamed compact and green with scale on scale,
But special burnishment adorned his mail
And special terror weighed upon his frown;

His punier brethren quaked before his tail,
Broad as a rafter, potent as a flail.
So he grew lord and master of his kin:
But who shall tell the tale of all their woes?
An execrable appetite arose,
He battened on them, crunched, and sucked them in.
He knew no law, he feared no binding law,
But ground them with inexorable jaw:
The luscious fat distilled upon his chin,
Exuded from his nostrils and his eyes,
While still like hungry death he fed his maw;
Till every minor crocodile being dead
And buried too, himself gorged to the full,
He slept with breath oppressed and unstrung claw.
Oh marvel passing strange which next I saw:
In sleep he dwindled to the common size,
And all the empire faded from his coat.
Then from far off a wingèd vessel came,
Swift as a swallow, subtle as a flame:
I know not what it bore of freight or host,
But white it was as an avenging ghost.
It levelled strong Euphrates in its course;
Supreme yet weightless as an idle mote
It seemed to tame the waters without force
Till not a murmur swelled or billow beat:
Lo, as the purple shadow swept the sands,
The prudent crocodile rose on his feet
And shed appropriate tears and wrung his hands.

What can it mean? you ask. I answer not
For meaning, but myself must echo, What?
And tell it as I saw it on the spot.

Gone for Ever

O happy rose-bud blooming
   Upon thy parent tree,—
Nay, thou art too presuming;
For soon the earth entombing
   Thy faded charms shall be,
And the chill damp consuming.

O happy skylark springing
   Up to the broad blue sky,
Too fearless in thy winging,
Too gladsome in thy singing,
   Thou also soon shalt lie
Where no sweet notes are ringing.

And through life's shine and shower
   We shall have joy and pain;
But in the summer bower,
And at the morning hour,
   We still shall look in vain
For the same bird and flower.

An End

Love, strong as Death, is dead.
Come, let us make his bed
Among the dying flowers:
A green turf at his head;
And a stone at his feet,
Whereon we may sit
In the quiet evening hours.

He was born in the Spring,
And died before the harvesting:
On the last warm Summer day
He left us; he would not stay
For Autumn twilight cold and gray.
Sit we by his grave, and sing
He is gone away.

To few chords and sad and low
Sing we so:
Be our eyes fixed on the grass
Shadow-veiled as the years pass,
While we think of all that was
In the long ago.

PENGUIN ARCHIVE

H. G. Wells *The Time Machine*
M. R. James *The Stalls of Barchester Cathedral*
Jane Austen *The History of England by a Partial, Prejudiced and Ignorant Historian*
Edgar Allan Poe *Hop-Frog*
Virginia Woolf *The New Dress*
Antoine de Saint-Exupéry *Night Flight*
Oscar Wilde *A Poet Can Survive Everything But a Misprint*
George Orwell *Can Socialists be Happy?*
Dorothy Parker *Horsie*
D. H. Lawrence *Odour of Chrysanthemums*
Homer *The Wrath of Achilles*
Emily Brontë *No Coward Soul Is Mine*
Romain Gary *Lady L.*
Charles Dickens *The Chimes*
Dante *Hell*
Georges Simenon *Stan the Killer*
F. Scott Fitzgerald *The Rich Boy*
Katherine Mansfield *A Dill Pickle*
Fyodor Dostoyevsky *The Dream of a Ridiculous Man*

Franz Kafka *A Hunger-Artist*
Leo Tolstoy *Family Happiness*
Karen Blixen *The Dreaming Child*
Federico García Lorca *Cicada!*
Vladimir Nabokov *Revenge*
Albert Camus *A Short Guide to Towns Without a Past*
Muriel Spark *The Driver's Seat*
Carson McCullers *Reflections in a Golden Eye*
Wu Cheng'en *Monkey King Makes Havoc in Heaven*
Friedrich Nietzsche *Ecce Homo*
Laurie Lee *A Moment of War*
Roald Dahl *Lamb to the Slaughter*
Frank O'Connor *The Genius*
James Baldwin *The Fire Next Time*
Hermann Hesse *Strange News from Another Planet*
Gertrude Stein *Paris France*
Seneca *Why I am a Stoic*
Snorri Sturluson *The Prose Edda*
Elizabeth Gaskell *Lois the Witch*
Sei Shōnagon *A Lady in Kyoto*
Yasunari Kawabata *Thousand Cranes*
Jack Kerouac *Tristessa*
Arthur Schnitzler *A Confirmed Bachelor*
Chester Himes *All God's Chillun Got Pride*

Bram Stoker *The Burial of the Rats*
Czesław Miłosz *Rescue*
Hans Christian Andersen *The Emperor's New Clothes*
Bohumil Hrabal *Closely Watched Trains*
Italo Calvino *Under the Jaguar Sun*
Stanislaw Lem *The Seventh Voyage*
Shirley Jackson *The Daemon Lover*
Stefan Zweig *Chess*
Kate Chopin *The Story of an Hour*
Allen Ginsberg *Sunflower Sutra*
Rabindranath Tagore *The Broken Nest*
Søren Kierkegaard *The Seducer's Diary*
Mary Shelley *Transformation*
Nikolai Leskov *Night Owls*
Willa Cather *A Lost Lady*
Emilia Pardo Bazán *The Lady Bandit*
W. B. Yeats *Sailing to Byzantium*
Margaret Cavendish *The Blazing World*
Lafcadio Hearn *Some Japanese Ghosts*
Sarah Orne Jewett *The Country of the Pointed Firs*
Vincent van Gogh *For Art and for Life*
Dylan Thomas *Do Not Go Gentle Into That Good Night*
Mikhail Bulgakov *A Dog's Heart*
Saadat Hasan Manto *The Price of Freedom*

Gérard de Nerval *October Nights*
Rumi *Where Everything is Music*
H. P. Lovecraft *The Shadow Out of Time*
Christina Rossetti *To Read and Dream*
Dambudzo Marechera *The House of Hunger*
Andy Warhol *Beauty*
Maurice Leblanc *The Escape of Arsène Lupin*
Eileen Chang *Jasmine Tea*
Irmgard Keun *After Midnight*
Walter Benjamin *Unpacking My Library*
Epictetus *Whatever is Rational is Tolerable*
Ota Pavel *How I Came to Know Fish*
César Aira *An Episode in the Life of a Landscape Painter*
Hafez *I am a Bird from Paradise*
Clarice Lispector *The Burned Sinner and the Harmonious Angels*
Maryse Condé *Tales from the Heart*
Audre Lorde *Coal*
Mary Gaitskill *Secretary*
Tove Ditlevsen *The Umbrella*
June Jordan *Passion*
Antonio Tabucchi *Requiem*
Alexander Lernet-Holenia *Baron Bagge*
Wang Xiaobo *The Maverick Pig*